THE OFFICIAL
CHELSEA FC
ANNUAL 2019

Written by David Antill, Richard Godden,
James Sugrue and Dominic Bliss

Designed by Jon Dalrymple

A Grange Publication

© 2018. Published by Grange Communications Ltd., Edinburgh,
under licence from Chelsea FC Merchandising Limited.
www.chelseafc.com. Printed in the EU.

Photography © Chelsea FC; Darren Walsh; Getty Images;
Press Association and Shutterstock. Chelsea logo and crest
are registered trademarks of Chelsea Football Club.

ISBN: 978-1-912595-04-4

WELCOME

to the 2019 Official Chelsea FC Annual!

You can find all you need to know about the Blues inside, with profiles on the manager and every player, as well as all the facts you could want about the club and our history.

We also look back on a record-breaking 2017/18 season across our men's, women's and Academy teams, reliving how we won the FA Cup for the eighth time, the Under-18s triumphed in every competition we entered and Chelsea Women claimed the Double. That made us the first club ever to lift the FA Cup, FA Youth Cup and Women's FA Cup in the same year.

Plus you can find out which members of the Blues squad are also talented in other sports and what the players liked doing when they were kids.

If that wasn't enough, there is the chance to prove you are Chelsea's biggest fan by showing off your knowledge in plenty of quizzes.

We hope you have fun reading!

Stamford and Bridget

CONTENTS

CUP CONQUERORS!

Chelsea celebrated becoming the first club in history to lift the FA Cup, Women's FA Cup and FA Youth Cup in the same season at the end of an action-packed 2017/18 campaign!

STORY OF THE SEASON

The Blues became FA Cup winners for the eighth time and, in doing so, secured a major trophy for the 10th season out of 15 since Roman Abramovich became the club's owner. Here are the key moments from the 2017/18 campaign:

Chelsea ended the season with victory at Wembley Stadium and we also made history at the start of it by winning the first Premier League match held at the ground. Marcos Alonso was the surprise hero against Spurs with two goals – and just look how much it meant to him!

Alvaro Morata scored his first hat-trick for Chelsea with a devastating display of finishing at the Britannia Stadium when we put four goals past Stoke City in September. It's the same in Spain as it is in England – you score a hat-trick and the matchball is all yours!

The Blues were back in the Champions League after a one-year absence and pundits were saying our win over Atletico Madrid was the best away performance in Europe by an English team in years! Substitute Michy Batshuayi was the hero when he scored the winner with the last kick of the game.

One of the best games of the season was our back-and-forth clash with Watford. Pedro scored a wonder goal but the hero was his fellow Spaniard Cesar Azpilicueta, who scored a late winner. Incredibly, all five of his Premier League goals have come against teams whose name begins with the letter W!

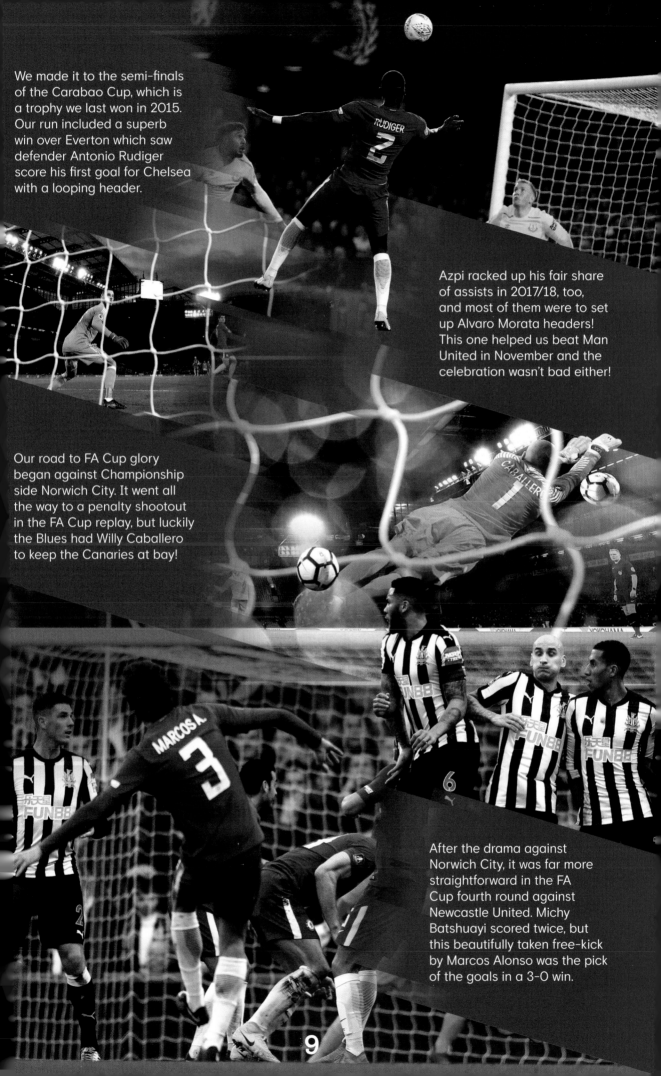

We made it to the semi-finals of the Carabao Cup, which is a trophy we last won in 2015. Our run included a superb win over Everton which saw defender Antonio Rudiger score his first goal for Chelsea with a looping header.

Azpi racked up his fair share of assists in 2017/18, too, and most of them were to set up Alvaro Morata headers! This one helped us beat Man United in November and the celebration wasn't bad either!

Our road to FA Cup glory began against Championship side Norwich City. It went all the way to a penalty shootout in the FA Cup replay, but luckily the Blues had Willy Caballero to keep the Canaries at bay!

After the drama against Norwich City, it was far more straightforward in the FA Cup fourth round against Newcastle United. Michy Batshuayi scored twice, but this beautifully taken free-kick by Marcos Alonso was the pick of the goals in a 3-0 win.

STORY OF THE SEASON

Hull City couldn't handle Willian, who was in sensational form in a Friday night FA Cup fifth round tie at the Bridge, scoring two goals. Pedro was also on the scoresheet, while Olivier Giroud grabbed his first Chelsea goal following his arrival in January.

The Brazilian was at it again on an electric night at Stamford Bridge when we took on Barcelona in the last 16 of the Champions League. If it hadn't been for Lionel Messi's first goal against Chelsea, which was completely against the run of play and gave Barca a crucial away goal, who knows how the rest of the tie would have panned out?

A tough FA Cup quarter-final tie away at Leicester City at a freezing King Power Stadium went to extra time after Alvaro Morata's first-half goal was cancelled out late on, but Pedro emerged from the bench to head the winner in extra time and send us to Wembley.

Victor Moses chipped in with some vital goals throughout the season, including the winner against Burnley at Turf Moor.

Olivier Giroud threw his name into the hat for Goal of the Season with a spectacular effort against Southampton in the FA Cup semi-final, tearing through their defence like a slalom skier before stabbing the ball home. Alvaro Morata's perfectly placed header secured the win which ensured we'd be returning to Wembley to contest our 13th FA Cup final.

Although our bid to qualify for the Champions League came up just short, this towering header from Olivier Giroud was enough to beat Liverpool, which is something that always goes down well with Blues supporters!

Chelsea took on Man United at Wembley with the FA Cup at stake – and the Blues emerged victorious thanks to Eden Hazard's ice-cool penalty after he'd been fouled by Phil Jones, followed by a rock-solid defensive performance.

That meant we lifted the FA Cup for the eighth time, something only two clubs can better. Soon they are going to need a bigger trophy cabinet at Stamford Bridge!

MAURIZIO SARRI

Maurizio Sarri was announced as Chelsea's new head coach ahead of the 2018/19 season after impressing during his time in Italy, particularly while in charge at Napoli. His side were known for playing exciting, attacking football and he led them to two second-place finishes in Serie A, as well as back into the Champions League.

After arriving at Stamford Bridge, he said:

"I am very happy to be coming to Chelsea and the Premier League. It is an exciting new period in my career. I hope we can provide some entertaining football for our fans and that we will be competing for trophies at the end of the season, which is what this club deserves."

Did you know?

Sarri is the sixth Italian to take charge of the Blues, following on from Gianluca Vialli, Claudio Ranieri, Carlo Ancelotti, Roberto Di Matteo and Antonio Conte.

He was voted Serie A Coach of the Year in 2017.

Under Sarri, Napoli had the second best defence in Serie A for the last two seasons.

His nickname while he was manager of Sansovino was "Mr 33", because that is the number of set-pieces he prepared for his players.

Welcome home

Sarri's arrival at Chelsea saw the return of a club legend, with Gianfranco Zola joining as his assistant. Zola is one of our greatest players of all time, having wowed fans with his amazing skills and unbelievable goals during seven years with the Blues, when he scored 80 times in 311 appearances.

He has managed West Ham, Watford and Birmingham City and he is excited to be back with the club he loves.

"For me it is an amazing thing," he said. "I am very willing to work hard because it is going to be a difficult challenge but I am pleased to be here. It would be great to be successful with Maurizio and for the club and I will give my best, as I did in the past as a player."

Did you know?

Zola was named Chelsea's Player of the Year in 1999 and 2003, and also won the Football Writers' award at the end of his first season with the Blues.

He scored our winner in the 1998 European Cup Winners' Cup final against Stuttgart, just seconds after coming off the bench.

He last played for Chelsea a couple of months before joining us as a coach – as part of a Legends side who played Inter Milan at Stamford Bridge!

PLAYER PROFILES

Goalkeepers

KEPA ARRIZABALAGA

Date of birth: **03.10.94**
Nationality: **Spanish**
Signed from: **Athletic Bilbao**
Chelsea appearances: **0**
Clean sheets: **0**

DID YOU KNOW?
Kepa played in goal for Spain when they won the European Under-19 Championship in 2012.

WILLY CABALLERO

Date of birth: **28.09.81**
Nationality: **Argentinean**
Signed from: **Manchester City**
Chelsea appearances: **13**
Clean sheets: **5**

DID YOU KNOW?
Willy made his international debut for Argentina in March 2018 at the age of 36 and followed it up by starting in goal for all their games at the World Cup in Russia.

ROB GREEN

Date of birth: **18.01.80**
Nationality: **English**
Signed from: **Free agent**
Chelsea appearances: **0**
Clean sheets: **0**

DID YOU KNOW?
Rob made his 600th league appearance in 2017 during his time with Leeds United against his former club QPR.

Defenders

MARCOS ALONSO

Date of birth: **28.12.90**
Nationality: **Spanish**
Signed from: **Fiorentina**
Chelsea appearances: **81**
Goals: **14**

DID YOU KNOW?
Marcos has previously played in the Premier League for Bolton and Sunderland. When he was at Bolton he was team-mates with Gary Cahill. At Sunderland he was managed by Blues legend Gus Poyet.

ETHAN AMPADU

Date of birth: **14.09.00**
Nationality: **Welsh**
Signed from: **Exeter City**
Chelsea appearances: **7**
Goals: **0**

DID YOU KNOW?
Ethan became the first player born this century to represent Chelsea when he made his senior debut against Nottingham Forest in the Carabao Cup last season. He is the second youngest player to represent us in the Premier League.

CESAR AZPILICUETA

Date of birth: **28.08.89**
Nationality: **Spanish**
Signed from: **Marseille**
Chelsea appearances: **280**
Goals: **8**

DID YOU KNOW?
In 2017/18, Cesar played the most minutes of any Chelsea player for the third season running.

GARY CAHILL

Date of birth: **1912.85**
Nationality: **English**
Signed from: **Bolton Wanderers**
Chelsea appearances: **282**
Goals: **25**

DID YOU KNOW?
Since joining Chelsea in January 2012, Cahill has won six major honours with the Blues – the Champions League, Europa League, two Premier League titles, the FA Cup and League Cup.

ANDREAS CHRISTENSEN

Date of birth: **10.04.96**
Nationality: **Danish**
Signed from: **Chelsea Academy**
Chelsea appearances: **43**
Goals: **0**

DID YOU KNOW?
After achieving success with our Academy, Andreas has two Premier League winner's medals and has won the FA Cup and League Cup since progressing to our first team.

DAVID LUIZ

Date of birth: **22.04.87**
Nationality: **Brazilian**
Signed from: **Paris Saint-Germain**
Chelsea appearances: **198**
Goals: **15**

DID YOU KNOW?
David Luiz played as a forward when he was a boy, and offered to switch to the back for a game when his team were short of defenders.

PLAYER PROFILES

EMERSON PALMIERI

Date of birth: **03.08.94**
Nationality: **Italian**
Signed from: **Roma**
Chelsea appearances: **7**
Goals: **0**

DID YOU KNOW?
Emerson made his first-team debut for Brazilian club Sao Paulo at the age of 16.

ANTONIO RÜDIGER

Date of birth: **03.03.93**
Nationality: **German**
Signed from: **Roma**
Chelsea appearances: **45**
Goals: **3**

DID YOU KNOW?
Toni was named Man of the Match in the 2018 FA Cup final, as his solid performance in our defence helped us beat Manchester United.

DAVIDE ZAPPACOSTA

Date of birth: **11.06.92**
Nationality: **Italian**
Signed from: **Torino**
Chelsea appearances: **35**
Goals: **2**

DID YOU KNOW?
Davide's first goal for Chelsea was a long-range stunner on his full debut in our 6-0 Champions League win over Qarabag.

Midfielders

ROSS BARKLEY

Date of birth: **05.12.93**
Nationality: **English**
Signed from: **Everton**
Chelsea appearances: **4**

DID YOU KNOW?
Ross scored Everton's Goal of the Season in 2013/14, the same season he was named on the shortlist for the PFA Young Player of the Year awar...

DANNY DRINKWATER

Date of birth: **05.03.90**
Nationality: **English**
Signed from: **Leicester City**
Chelsea appearances: **22**
Goals: **1**

DID YOU KNOW?

Drinkwater came through Manchester United's youth ranks and was loaned to Huddersfield, Cardiff, Watford and Barnsley, before becoming a Premier League champion during a five-year spell with Leicester City.

CESC FÀBREGAS

Date of birth: **04.05.87**
Nationality: **Spanish**
Signed from: **Barcelona**
Chelsea appearances: **182**
Goals: **21**

DID YOU KNOW?

Cesc played his 100th career Champions League match in our away game against Roma in October 2017.

EDEN HAZARD

Date of birth: **07.01.91**
Nationality: **Belgian**
Signed from: **Lille**
Chelsea appearances: **300**
Goals: **90**

DID YOU KNOW?

Eden made his 300th appearance for the Blues in the 2018 FA Cup final and scored the winning goal from the penalty spot.

JORGINHO

Date of birth: **20.12.91**
Nationality: **Italian**
Signed from: **Napoli**
Chelsea appearances: **0**
Goals: **0**

DID YOU KNOW?

In Europe's big five leagues last season, no player had more touches of the ball per minute than Jorginho.

N'GOLO KANTÉ

Date of birth: **29.03.91**
Nationality: **French**
Signed from: **Leicester City**
Chelsea appearances: **89**
Goals: **3**

DID YOU KNOW?

Since moving to English football in 2015, N'Golo has won the Premier League twice, the FA Cup and, in 2018, became a World Cup winner with France. He was also a runner up at the 2016 European Championship

PLAYER PROFILES

MATEO KOVACIC

Date of birth: **06.05.94**
Nationality: **Croatian**
Signed from: **Real Madrid (loan)**
Chelsea appearances: **0**
Goals: **0**

DID YOU KNOW?

Mateo became one of the youngest players to score in the Champions League when he netted for Dynamo Zagreb against Lyon when he was 17.

RUBEN LOFTUS-CHEEK

Date of birth: **23.01.96**
Nationality: **English**
Signed from: **Chelsea Academy**
Chelsea appearances: **32**
Goals: **2**

DID YOU KNOW?

Ruben was scouted by Chelsea when he was seven years old and has been with the Blues since the Under-8s age group.

VICTOR MOSES

Date of birth: **12.12.90**
Nationality: **Nigerian**
Signed from: **Wigan Athletic**
Chelsea appearances: **122**
Goals: **18**

DID YOU KNOW?

In 2013, Moses won the Africa Cup of Nations with Nigeria and was voted his country's Player of the Year. He also represented the Super Eagles at the 2014 and 2018 World Cups.

PEDRO

Date of birth: **28.07.87**
Nationality: **Spanish**
Signed from: **Barcelona**
Chelsea appearances: **131**

DID YOU KNOW?

The 8,000th goal in all competitions over Chelsea's 112-year history was scored by Pedro in our 4-2 victory over Watford at Stamford Bridge in October 2017.

WILLIAN

Date of birth: **09.08.88**
Nationality: **Brazilian**
Signed from: **Anzhi Makhachkala**
Chelsea appearances: **236**
Goals: **44**

DID YOU KNOW?

Willian won the club's Goal of the Season in 2017/18 as well as being named Players' Player of the Year for the second time, having also won that award in 2016 when the fans named him as our best player as well.

Forwards

OLIVIER GIROUD

Date of birth: **30.09.86**
Nationality: **French**
Signed from: **Arsenal**
Chelsea appearances: **18**
Goals: **5**

DID YOU KNOW?

Olivier won the prestigious FIFA Puskas award in 2017 for goal of the year after his remarkable strike for Arsenal against Crystal Palace.

CALLUM HUDSON-ODOI

Date of birth: **07.11.00**
Nationality: **English**
Signed from: **Chelsea Academy**
Chelsea appearances: **4**
Goals: **0**

DID YOU KNOW?

Callum was one of six Chelsea Academy products to make thteir senior debut during the 2017/18 season.

ALVARO MORATA

Date of birth: **23.10.92**
Nationality: **Spanish**
Signed from: **Real Madrid**
Chelsea appearances: **48**
Goals: **15**

DID YOU KNOW?

Morata became a dad for the first time shortly before the start of the 2018/19 season when his wife gave birth to twins.

All stats correct at the end of the 2017/18 season

WHO AM I?

How well do you know your Blues heroes? We've put togethe a series of fiendish clues and it is up to you to match each on to the Chelsea first-team player pictured on the right.

1 My first FA Cup final was when we beat Manchester United in the final at Wembley, and I was chosen as Man of the Match for helping us keep a clean sheet!

2 I once played in three Champions League finals in four years, winning twice – but I lost the one that I scored in!

3 When we won the Premier League in 2016/17 I took home the Goal of the Month award twice, after scoring worldies against Spurs and Everton!

4 When Chelsea played Spurs in the first Premier League game at Wembley, I was the hero by scoring both our goals in a 2-1 win!

5 I don't really like awards ceremonies, which is a bit of a problem for me as I've won a whole host of personal honours since I joined Chelsea in 2016!

6 My final goal of the 2017/18 season came from the penalty spot and I've now converted more spot-kicks for Chelsea than everyone else apart from Frank Lampard!

7 As of the start of the 2018/19 campaign, all five of my Premier League goals have had something in common – they've all come against sides whose name begins with a W!

8 Although I come from an extremely hot country, I played in Ukraine and Russia before joining Chelsea!

9 My dad was signed by Brondby to replace the legendary goalkeeper Peter Schmeichel when he signed for Man United!

10 Before I signed for Chelsea I won the Puskas award in 2017, which is given to the player who scores the best goal in the world that year!

Answers on p62

ALONSO

AZPILICUETA

GIROUD

CHRISTENSEN

KANTE

PEDRO

HAZARD

RUDIGER

WILLIAN

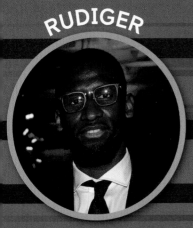

MORATA

LOVE AT FIRST SIGHT

We take a look at how famous Chelsea fans fell for the Blues.

Joe Wicks

Joe Wicks is famous around the world as fitness guru The Body Coach.

In the spring of 2018, he held a workout on the pitch at Stamford Bridge – the first event of its kind to take place at a football stadium – for more than 1,000 people and it was a dream come true after he grew up supporting the Blues.

"I've been a fan since I was about 10 years old," he explained. "I grew up in Epsom and we used to go to Kingstonian and watch the friendly game there every year. This was when the likes of Gianfranco Zola, Gianluca Vialli and Roberto Di Matteo were playing. I've also been to Cobham and met John Terry when he was playing here. He's a legend and a great inspiration."

It's not just former players that Joe has met, either, and he admits he would love to put one of our current greats through his paces. "I met Eden Hazard at the Chelsea Awards at the end of the season, he is such a lovely guy, very warm and friendly, so it would have been lovely to see him here!"

George Groves
Boxing world champion

I went to school in Fulham, not a million miles from Stamford Bridge, and the vast majority of my friends were Chelsea fans. Growing up around there it was either Chelsea or Fulham, and I didn't fancy Fulham, so I was Chelsea from an early age. It was good having so many Chelsea supporters in my class, we heavily outnumbered the Fulham fans.

Marvin Humes
DJ

My dad is a Chelsea fan. He's friends with Paul Elliott, who used to play for the club, and he took me to Paul's testimonial in 1995. At nine or 10 years old I was still a bit of a neutral football fan, but after I went to that game I fell in love with the Bridge, the atmosphere and the fans – from that day forward I was a Blue.

Tom and Sam Curran
England cricketers

Tom: I started supporting Chelsea when we moved over from Zimbabwe. I came to my first Premier League game about six years ago at Stamford Bridge and from then on this place just felt like home. Playing cricket for Surrey, who are based at the Oval, and being so close to Stamford Bridge, is obviously a big factor in allowing us to come along to games.

Sam: When I came over here, a lot of my schoolmates were Chelsea fans. Some of their dads had season tickets, so I was lucky enough to come to a few games with them and that's how I became a fan.

Tubes
Soccer AM Star

When I popped out of my mum! One of the first photos taken of me was with Stamford the Lion. My whole family are Chelsea fans, and my mum and dad made the local papers because they were the first people to have their wedding reception at Stamford Bridge, with a marquee on the pitch and everything!

ACADEMY:
CLEAN SWEEP!

Chelsea's Under-18s won an unprecedented Quadruple in 2017/18, going one trophy better than the previous season by winning all four of the competitions they entered. Solid at the back and lethal up front, the young Blues were unstoppable as they won the regional and national league titles, the first-ever Under-18s Premier League Cup and a fifth FA Youth Cup in a row. Let's take a look back at a season to remember for Chelsea's youngsters.

Chelsea have now won the FA Youth Cup five times in a row, equalling a record set by Manchester United way back in the 1950s. Last season's success was also our seventh in nine years in the famous old youth competition, showing just how strong our Academy has been in the last decade.

The 2017/18 final was a London derby against Arsenal, and although we played the first leg at home, we actually fell behind at Stamford Bridge and went in a goal down at half-time. However, we fired back with two goals from Dutch striker Daishawn Redan and another from defender Marc Guehi to give ourselves a 3-1 lead going into the away leg at Arsenal.

At the Emirates Stadium, we were in fine form, winning 4-0 thanks to goals from Scottish midfielder Billy Gilmour, a double from Callum Hudson-Odoi and one more from substitute Tino Anjorin. That meant a 7-1 win on aggregate – and time to party!

The Final

First Leg

Chelsea 3 (Redan 2, Guehi)

Arsenal 1 (Amaechi)

Chelsea (4-2-3-1): Cumming; Lamptey (Castillo 85), James (c), Guehi, Panzo; Gallagher, Gilmour; Uwakwe (Sterling h/t), McEachran, Hudson-Odoi; C Brown (Redan 61)

Second Leg

Arsenal 0

Chelsea 4 (Gilmour, Hudson-Odoi 2, Anjorin)

Chelsea (3-4-2-1): Cumming; James (c), Guehi, Panzo; Sterling, Gallagher (Mola 61), Gilmour, Castillo; McEachran (Anjorin 61), Hudson-Odoi; Redan (C Brown 71)

CADEMY: LEAN SWEEP!

...der-18s Premier League is divided into two parts. Firstly, clubs have to compete in a regional ... either the northern or the southern section, depending on where they are based. The winners of ...thern and southern section then play off for the national title, and in 2017/18 Chelsea successfully ...ed both their southern section title and the national championship, adding a league double to ...ouble cup success.

...eeing off the challenge of Arsenal and Southampton to win the southern section with just two ...s in 22 games, the young Blues went on to beat Manchester United 3-0 in the national final. Our ...corers on the night were Dujon Sterling, Billy Gilmour and Tariq Lamptey.

...s a fitting send-off for Jody Morris, who left his post as Under-18s coach at the end of the ...on to join his former Chelsea team-mate Frank Lampard on the first-team coaching staff ...erby County.

...an outstanding achievement to produce in big games, continually," Morris said at the ...of the 2017/18 campaign. "It's not easy to win these big games and to have won every ...hy we've entered this season just shows what a good group they are."

Taking On The Big Boys

Our Under-18s weren't the only Chelsea Academy side enjoying cup competitions last season. Our development squad also had two impressive cup runs, in two different age groups.

The first came in the Checkatrade Trophy, which is a cup competition for clubs in League One and League Two, but they also invite some Under-23 teams to enter, and Chelsea became the first Academy side to reach the semi-finals this season. To reach the last four, they beat the first teams of Exeter City, MK Dons, Portsmouth and Oxford United and they only lost the semi-final on a penalty shootout, against Lincoln.

"This year we played seven Football League teams and not one of them beat us over 90 minutes, and those games are priceless experience for lads of 17 or 18 years of age." said their proud coach, Joe Edwards.

He was also in charge of the Chelsea Under-19s team who reached the final of the UEFA Youth League, which is a youth version of the Champions League. We saw off Atletico Madrid, Roma, Qarabag, Feyenoord, Real Madrid and Porto to get to the final, but were unfortunate to lose 3-0 to Barcelona and finish as runners-up.

All in all, it was another thrilling season for the Academy. Here's hoping there's more to come!

1,000 PREMIER LEAGUE GAMES

Chelsea's last game of the 2017/18 season was also our 1,000th Premier League game. Let's take a look at some of the best facts and figures from our league form between 1992 and 2018...

THE NUMBERS*

The top tier of English football was renamed the Premier League in 1992, and of the 26 seasons played since the Premier League began, Chelsea have finished top five times. At the end of last season, we played our 1,000th game in the competition, and as you can see we have won way more than we have lost...

PL GAMES	WINS	DRAWS	DEFEATS	GOALS SCORED	GOALS CONCEDED	CLEAN SHEETS
1,000	537	248	215	1,707	963	404

IN THE BEGINNING

Our first-ever Premier League game was against Oldham Athletic on 15 August 1992. It was a 1-1 draw at Stamford Bridge and the first Chelsea goalscorer of the new era of English football was Mick Harford (pictured), who was known to be a proper hard man! Oldham played the first two Premier League seasons before they were relegated in 1994, but they now play in League Two. In fact, Chelsea are one of only six clubs to have played in the division since it began.

WINS

We've had some unforgettable victories in those 1,000 Premier League games but what were the biggest ones?

Biggest Chelsea home wins

8-0 Wigan - May 2010

8-0 Aston Villa - December 2012

Biggest Chelsea away wins

6-0 Barnsley - August 1997

6-0 Wigan - August 2010

RECORD HOLDERS

Who has played the most Premier League games for Chelsea? Here are the top five:

492	John Terry
429	Frank Lampard
333	Petr Cech
261	Branislav Ivanovic
261	Dennis Wise

What about Chelsea's top Premier League goalscorers? How many of the top five do you remember?

147	Frank Lampard
104	Didier Drogba
69	Jimmy Floyd Hasselbaink
69*	Eden Hazard
59	Gianfranco Zola

Now one for the goalkeepers among you. Here are the Chelsea keepers with the most Premier League clean sheets:

166	Petr Cech
62	Carlo Cudicini
49	Thibaut Courtois
47	Ed De Goey
38	Dmitri Kharine

* All statistics correct up to July 2018

FACT OR FICTION?

There have been some strange events over the course of Chelsea's history, sometimes so strange that you couldn't have made it up. However, can you tell which of these 10 stories really happened, and which ones we have just made up for fun?

1

FACT ○ FICTION ○

Chelsea first changed our shorts to match our blue shirts in the Sixties, to help colour-blind goalkeeper Peter Bonetti tell his defenders and the opposition's strikers apart, with most teams wearing white shorts at the time.

2

FACT ○ FICTION ○

Marcos Alonso is the third generation of his family to play football for the Spanish national team, with his dad and granddad both international players, and also named Marcos Alonso.

3

FACT ○ FICTION ○

Jorginho and Emerson have been team-mates at international tournaments for two different countries, both travelling to the Under-20 World Cup with Brazil before being called up to Italy's senior squad for Euro 2016.

4

FACT ○ FICTION ○

Our biggest-ever win was 13-0 against Jeunesse Hautcharage in the 1971/72 European Cup Winners' Cup, but the score wasn't the most surprising thing about the game, as our opponents from Luxembourg lined up with a one-armed man in their team.

5

FACT ● FICTION ●

Didier Drogba played one match for Chelsea as a goalkeeper, against Barcelona in the 2006/07 Champions League group stage, after Petr Cech, Carlo Cudicini and Henrique Hilario were all injured in the space of a week.

6

FACT ● FICTION ●

We all know Stamford the Lion and Bridget the Lioness, but our original club mascot was a giant Chelsea bun, before Stamford made his first appearance in the Eighties.

7

FACT ● FICTION ●

Eden Hazard was on a top-flight football pitch before he was even born, with his mother playing in the Belgian first division while she was pregnant.

8

FACT ● FICTION ●

Chelsea owes its existence to a badly behaved dog, as Stamford Bridge's owner Gus Mears started the club to say sorry for his pet biting a football fan friend, Fred Parker.

9

FACT ● FICTION ●

We won our first FA Cup in 1970, but we could have lifted the trophy over 50 years earlier if they had penalty shootouts in those days, as we lost the 1915 final on the luck of a coin toss after a 0-0 draw against Sheffield United.

10

FACT ● FICTION ●

In the early days of our existence we played two first-team games on the same day, beating Burnley 1-0 in the league but losing 7-1 to Crystal Palace in the FA Cup.

Answers on p62

ROY BENTLEY

1924-2018

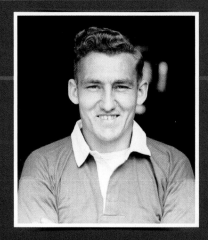

In 2018, Chelsea lost two club legends, Ray Wilkins and Roy Bentley. We take a look at why they will always be heroes to the Stamford Bridge faithful...

The Player

Roy Bentley was a superstar striker for Chelsea in the 1950s. He arrived at Stamford Bridge from Newcastle United in 1948 and before that he served in the Royal Navy during World War Two.

He stayed at Chelsea for more than eight years, and scored 150 goals, which was a club record at the time. Even today, only four players – Frank Lampard, Bobby Tambling, Kerry Dixon and Didier Drogba – have scored more.

Bentley's form also gained him a place in the England squad between 1949 and 1955, and he scored nine international goals in 12 caps. As a striker, he was strong, good at heading, had a powerful shot and many people talked about his clever movement off the ball. He goes down in history as one of the greatest players ever to pull on a Chelsea shirt.

In 1954/55, Bentley was our captain when Chelsea won the league for the first time ever. It was a special year to do it too, because the club was celebrating its 50th anniversary that year. Roy was the main man up front that season as well. He scored 21 goals, including a hat-trick against his old team, Newcastle, in a 4-3 win.

50 years later, when we won our next league title, he came out onto the pitch with his team-mates from 1955, carrying the Premier League trophy, and the old First Division trophy they had won all those years earlier. They were cheered to the rafters by everyone in the stadium.

If you look carefully at the banners that hang behind the goals at Stamford Bridge, you will see that one of them has BENTLEY'S BOYS written on it, next to a portrait of Roy. It just goes to show how important he was to the Chelsea supporters that even now, more than 60 years after he led us to that first league title, his name is still known at the place he once lit up with his wonderful goals.

RAY 'BUTCH' WILKINS
ONE OF OUR OW
1956 – 2018

RAY WILKINS
1956-2018

The Player

Ray Wilkins first started playing for Chelsea's youth system as a 10-year-old and made his way through the age groups to become a first-team player at the age of 17, in October 1973. A year later, he was captain, which just shows how highly rated he was by the club's management. In his time at Chelsea, we were not one of the top teams in the country, and he had to pick us up after relegation in 1975 and help steer the team back to the top division. He did so brilliantly.

He was an attacking midfielder, who passed the ball perfectly and scored a few goals too. He played at least 207 times and scored 34 goals, but most importantly he was the crowd's favourite player.

After leaving Chelsea in 1979, Ray went on to play for Manchester United, AC Milan, PSG, Rangers and Queens Park Rangers, as well as several other clubs in his later career. He also earned 84 England caps, and even became captain of the national team, but it all began at Chelsea, his spiritual home, and he returned to Stamford Bridge many years later.

When he retired from playing, Wilkins became a coach and he worked at several clubs, including Chelsea, where he returned in 1998 to work with our manager at the time, Gianluca Vialli.

Ray was assistant manager when we won the last FA Cup final at the original Wembley stadium in 2000 and, after leaving to work elsewhere for a few years, came back again in 2008 to be assistant manager to Luiz Felipe Scolari and then Guus Hiddink as we won the FA Cup again. The last Chelsea manager he worked under was Carlo Ancelotti, who he helped to win the Premier League and FA Cup Double in the 2009/10 season. Ancelotti loved having Ray by his side and once explained how much the club meant to him.

> "Ray is one of those select few, always present, noble in spirit, a real blue-blood, Chelsea flows in his veins."
>
> Carlo Ancelotti

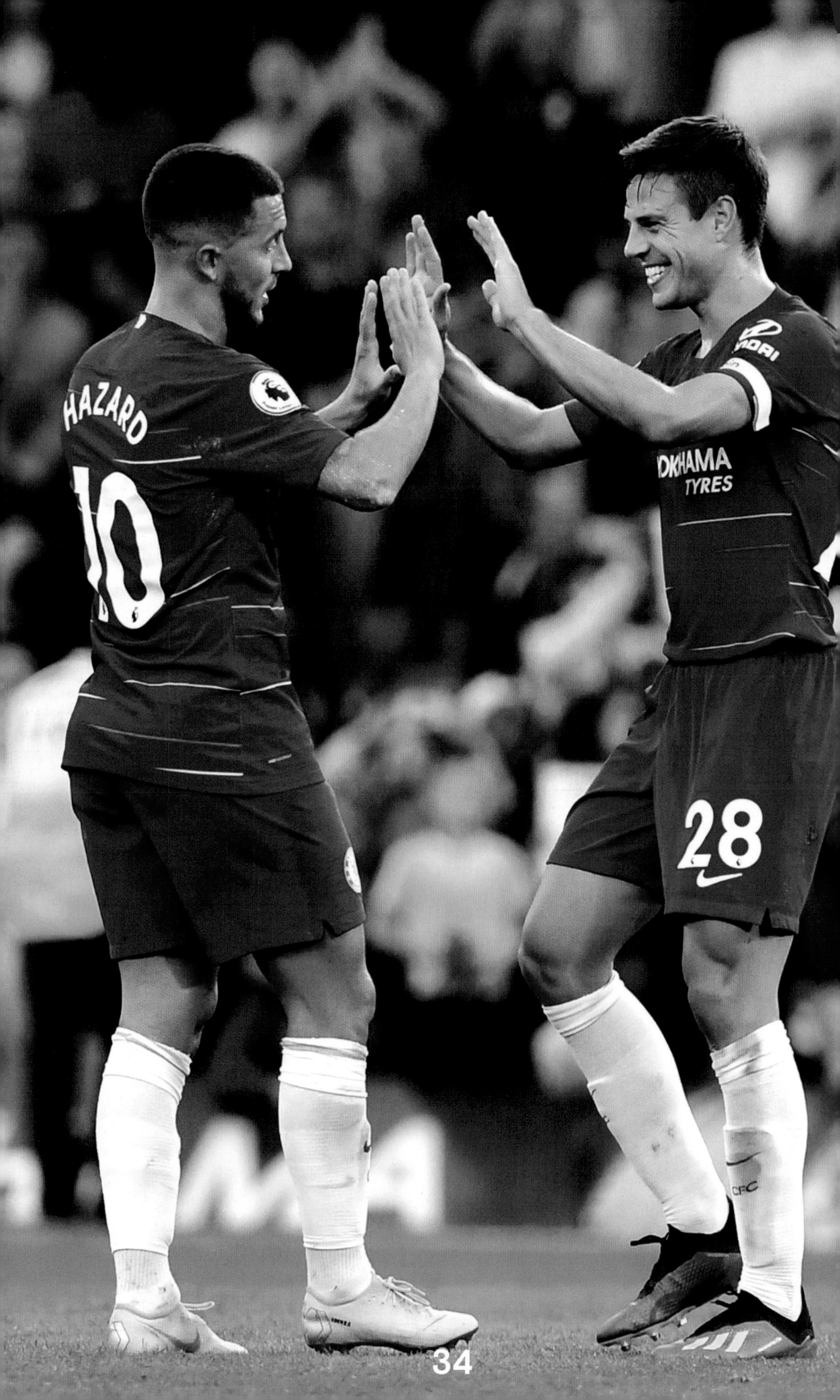
HAZARD
10
TYRES
28

WORLD BEATERS

While most people were off enjoying their summer holiday, plenty of Chelsea players spent their summer in Russia competing for international football's biggest prize, the World Cup.

Allez les Bleus

It was France who became the stars of the show, with N'Golo Kanté and Olivier Giroud both playing in every game as they went all the way to the final, where they beat Croatia 4-2 in Moscow to get their hands on the famous gold trophy.

Super Eagles

Nigeria failed to make it out of a tough group including Argentina and finalists Croatia, but Victor Moses did get himself a World Cup goal in their 2-1 defeat to the South Americans. Defender Kenneth Omeruo also played in two of their matches.

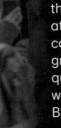

Samba boys

Willian started all five of Brazil's games as one of the best supported teams at the tournament. They comfortably topped their group on their way to the quarter-finals, where he was stopped by some of his Belgian Chelsea team-mates.

Golden generation

Belgium had more Blues in their squad than any other team, Eden Hazard, Thibaut Courtois and Michy Batshuayi coming home to a heroes' welcome after the country's best-ever result at a World Cup. Captain Hazard got his third goal of the tournament as they won the third-place play-off against England. Batshuayi also found the net, against Tunisia in the group stage, and Courtois was given the Golden Glove award for the best goalkeeper.

Lions' pride

Gary Cahill and Ruben Loftus-Cheek were part of the England squad that reached the semi-finals, equalling their best foreign World Cup. It was definitely a summer to remember for Loftus-Cheek, who made his competitive international debut in their first game, a win over Tunisia, making four appearances in total.

HEADS WE WIN

Chelsea led the way with headed goals in the Premier League in the 2017/18, with 17 of our tally of 62 coming as a result of our players using their noggin to good effect! We highlight which Blues made the most of their team-mates' pin-point crossing, plus we've picked out a few of our all-time favourite Chelsea headers.

Alvaro Morata scored seven headers in his debut season in the English top flight, a tally which has been bettered by only four players in a single Premier League campaign: Dwight Yorke, Roque Santa Cruz, Dion Dublin (all 8) and Duncan Ferguson (9). Shout-out to his compatriot, Cesar Azpilicueta, who set up six of Morata's Premier League goals last season – that's how you help your mate settle in!

Two newly promoted sides were on the receiving end of Marcos Alonso headers last term as he netted against Brighton and Huddersfield, and he was one of three Blues to end the campaign with two headed goals, along with Olivier Giroud and Antonio Rudiger.

Peter Osgood – 1970 FA Cup final v Leeds United

Of the other headed goalscorers, Michy Batshuayi and Cesar Azpilicueta both scored theirs in our thrilling 4-2 win over Watford, Tiemoue Bakayoko nodded one in against Crystal Palace and Willian netted a rare header in our win at Huddersfield.

Didier Drogba – 2012 Champions League final v Bayern Munich

Branislav Ivanovic – 2013 Europa League final v Benfica

Each year, at the Cobham training ground, players and staff get together to play a pool tournament, and this year's winner was N'Golo Kanté – who else?

The French midfield dynamo is not the first sporting all-rounder to pull on a Chelsea shirt, though. Far from it. You know those people who are just annoyingly good at whatever sport they turn their hands to? Well, it turns out loads of them have passed through Stamford Bridge. Let's take a look at some of the greats.

JOHN TERRY

JT grew up playing snooker with his dad and his uncle and his skills with the cue came in handy during his days at Chelsea, when he was a regular in the pool tournament final, winning it on several occasions. He got the chance to take on the ultimate test when former world snooker champion Neil Robertson visited the training ground in November 2013. The pair played a couple of frames on the Cobham pool table – where the baize is blue, naturally – and won one game each. In fact, JT potted every ball to win his frame, leaving the snooker champ a little bit red-faced! "He was a lot better than I expected!" Robertson laughed, relieved at taking the second frame to level things up.

MAX WOOSNAM

Back in March 1914, when Chelsea Football Club was just nine years old, a centre-half called Max Woosnam showed up at Stamford Bridge on a short-term deal. He played three games, and we kept a clean sheet in all of them, but then he had to go back to Cambridge University to finish his studies. He wasn't just a top student at school, though, he had the skills on the playing fields too. Woosnam hit 144 not out in a cricket game at Lord's, managed a maximum 147 break on the snooker table and played football for England. Just to rub it in, he won a Gold Medal at the 1920 Olympics, playing tennis! That's right, Woosnam was the Great Britain Davis Cup captain. It was like rolling John Terry, Andy Murray, Ronnie O'Sullivan and Alistair Cook into one! Well, sort of.

ROUNDERS

ANDRIY SHEVCHENKO

...ts of footballers like to play a round of golf in their spare ...me, none more so than Andriy Shevchenko, the Ukrainian ...ternational and winner of the 2004 Ballon d'Or for the ...est footballer in Europe. He spent two years at Chelsea ...etween 2006 and 2008, but when he eventually retired ...rom football, he decided to turn his hobby into his job and ...became a professional golfer. In September 2013, 'Sheva' – as he was nicknamed – took part in a Challenge Tour event in his home country and was an ambassador for Team Europe at the 2018 Ryder Cup in Paris! Amazingly, he isn't even the first ex-Chelsea player to become a professional golfer. American striker Roy Wegerle, who played for Chelsea between 1986 and 1988, hit the golf course hard after he retired from football, and even competed on the European Tour in 2002. After playing in his first pro golf event he said, "I don't think I was ever as nervous at Wembley!"

BEN HOWARD BAKER

The only goalkeeper to score a goal for Chelsea, Ben Howard Baker played for the Blues for five years between 1921 and 1926. His goal was a penalty, and his decision to come forward to take it showed how much confidence he had in his sporting prowess. Like Max Woosnam, he also played tennis at Wimbledon, but his most impressive achievements came in athletics, where he competed in the 1912 and 1920 Olympics and held the British high jump record for a quarter of a century.

FRANK LAMPARD

JT wasn't the only Chelsea player of his generation who could have been a contender in another sporting field. As a schoolboy, Frank Lampard was almost as comfortable with a cricket bat in his hands as he was with a ball at his feet, as you can tell from this photo with England cricket legend Kevin Pietersen. He even represented his county at youth level. "I played cricket for Essex and played it through until the end of my schooldays," Lamps told the Chelsea programme back in 2009. "I was decent at most sports, I was very sporty and tried to take part in all the sports going on at school."

CHELSEA FC WOMEN

Chelsea FC Women are the top club in England once again after securing our second league and FA Cup Double in three seasons. We look back at an incredible 2017/18 campaign for the Blues and give you more than a few reasons to go and see them in action this year.

WOMEN'S FA CUP WINNERS 2018

Ramona Bachmann lit up the FA Cup final at Wembley in front of a competition record 45,000 supporters at Wembley Stadium, netting a sensational brace to help us to a 3-1 victory over Arsenal. The tricky forward comes from Switzerland and it just so happens that Roberto Di Matteo, who scored in two FA Cup finals for Chelsea's men's team, was also born there!

There was a brief cause for tension when Arsenal pulled a goal back, but it didn't last long as Super Fran Kirby put us 3-1 up and as good as wrote our name on the trophy.

For captain Katie Chapman it was the 10th time she has won the Women's FA Cup in her incredible career, the first of which came when she was 14 years old. The skipper shared the moment of lifting the trophy with Maren Mjelde.

WOMEN'S SUPER LEAGUE 1 CHAMPIONS 2017/

No one could dispute Chelsea Women's status as the top si in England after we went through the whole WSL1 campaign unbeaten. The Blues were in great form from the word go, hammering Bristol City on the opening day of the season, a we rarely let our foot off the gas from then.

There were incredible wins over Arsenal and Birmingham City along the way at Kingsmeadow, which included goalscoring contributions from Maren Mjelde and Erin Cuthbert, with the latter earning a deserved nomination for the PFA Women's Young Player of the Year award.

The title was clinched in the penultimate round of fixtures w Jonna Andersson, a mid-season signing from Sweden, put the seal on a 2-0 victory over Bri

Incredibly, we looked like losing our unbeaten record on the final day of the campaign when we went 2-0 down against Liverpool in no time at all, but two brilliant goal from Ji So-Yun helped inspire a turnaround which meant we t were the WSL1's Invincibles.

WOMEN'S CHAMPIONS LEAGUE SEMI-FINALISTS

The Blues reached the semi-finals of the Women's Champions League for the first time in the club's history – and the run to the last four could hardly have been any tougher! We started off against Bayern Munich, when Fran Kirby's goal in the second leg proved so vital in sealing our progress on away goals in an unforgettable tie. We then beat Rosengard and Montpellier, when Erin Cuthbert's late goal in the south of France helped us through. However, Wolfsburg proved too strong in the semi-finals and it's the third season in a row we've been knocked out by the German club!

PFA TEAM
OF THE YEAR

The PFA WSL1 Team of the Year was packed full of Chelsea Women's players! No fewer than five of them were selected in the XI: **Millie Bright, Hannah Blundell, Maren Mjelde, Ji So-Yun and Fran Kirby.** If you ask us, that's a pretty good five-a-side team – who'd need a goalkeeper with that much quality on the pitch?!

FRAN-TASTIC KIRBY!

It was a collective effort behind Chelsea's success in 2017/18, with the whole squad playing their part in making it an unforgettable year, but the contribution made by Fran Kirby resulted in the England star winning a whole host of individual honours. She's pictured here winning the Chelsea Women's Player of the Year award, but on top of that she also took home the FWA and PFA Women's Footballer of the Year honours. In the PFA vote there were five Chelsea players on the shortlist of six, which shows just how dominant we were last season!

CHELSEA FC WOMEN

MUM OF THE YEAR

May 2018 was an incredible month on the pitch for Emma Hayes as her side won two trophies and she was chosen as LMA Manager of the Year – but it was even better away from the football field. The Chelsea Women's boss became a mother for the first time, giving birth to baby Harry. Here he is on his first trip to Stamford Bridge!

ONCE A BLUE, ALWAYS A BLUE...

Chelsea Women said goodbye to a few players wh had a big role to play in our first trophy successes, including the long-serving Claire Rafferty, who spe 11 years with us, and striker Eniola Aluko, who is the club's all-time leading scorer. Katie Chapman also ended her professional career, which lasted more than 20 years and saw her win just about every trophy going!

FIRST OF MANY

Drew Spence scored the first goal by a Chelsea Women's player at Kingsmeadow when she headed home the opener in our 6-0 win over Bristol City to kick-off the 2017/18 WSL1 season.

TOP OF THE STOPS

Fans of Chelsea Women have known for years just how good Hedvig Lindahl is, but did you know she is officially the best goalkeeper in the world? Viggy was selected in the FIFPro Women's Team of the Year for 2018, which was the first time the Swede had been chosen in the best XI on the planet!

HOME SWEET HOME

Chelsea Women play their home matches at Kingsmeadow, which is in Kingston-upon-Thames and only a few miles away from Stamford Bridge. Tickets cost £3 for kids and £6 for adults. You can find more information on chelseafc.com.

Here's a sneak peek at what the girls have been up to in the past few months!

SOCIAL MEDIA

You can follow us across social media, where you'll get to see all the best goals, selfies, behind-the-scenes action and much more from your favourite Chelsea Women players!

Find us on:

 Facebook: /ChelseaFCW

 Twitter: @ChelseaFCW

 Instagram: @ChelseaFCW

I WAS SO PROUD. TO SCORE IN THE FIRST FA CUP FINAL AT WEMBLEY IS SOMETHING I AM SO HAPPY ABOUT.

JI SO-YUN

WIN THE CHANCE TO BE A MASCOT!

How would you like to be a mascot at a Chelsea Women's game at Kingsmeadow? If you are aged between six and 13 years old and would like to walk out with the players before a match, simply answer this question to be in with a chance of winning!

Which Chelsea Women's player scored twice in the 2018 FA Cup final?
A. Ramona Bachmann   B. Fran Kirby   C. Ji So-Yun

Entry is by email only. Only one entry per contestant. Please enter CFC MASCOT followed by either A, B, or C in the subject line of an email. In the body of the email, please include your full name, address, postcode, email address, phone number and date of birth and send to: frontdesk@grangecommunications.co.uk by Friday 29th March 2019.

WHEN WE WERE YOUNG

Chelsea's players reminisce about their childhoods, from favourite memories to important lessons they learned, and a few funny tales along the way.

FIRST TRICK

The nutmeg, for sure. I remember, when I used to watch football, I was always like, "Wow, nutmeg!" After I saw this skill, I wanted to do it all the time, even around the house. I remember trying to nutmeg my mum when she was walking past me. In France it is called a petit pont, which means "small bridge", because it's like putting the ball under the little bridge.

WISE WORDS

If I could give any advice to young people, I would tell them to always go to school, because you never know what will happen in your life and school can prepare you for anything.
So try to do well at school and then, if you dream of becoming a footballer or something like that, you need to try everything to make your dream come true. That's what I did.

Eden Hazard

I WISH I KNEW THAT

If I could give advice to myself as a boy, I would say to trust yourself, whether you fail or succeed. Keep learning. Give your best and see what happens, but be determined and give everything you have.

N'Golo Kanté

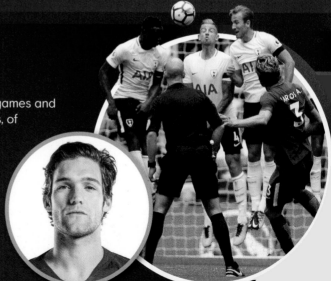

FIRST TRICK

I've never been a big fan of tricks. I just played games and tried to score goals. I liked to practice free-kicks, of course, and I would watch the players for the teams my father was coaching to learn how to take them well.

Marcos Alonso

THE BOY I USED TO BE

I used to speak a lot, and always about football! When someone came round to the house, I would always be speaking to them about football and I remember my big brothers saying, "You can have another conversation, you know!" But as a boy, I was always very happy, always running and always doing something.

Alvaro Morata

NICKNAME

It was "Chaussettes", which is French for "Socks". My brothers loved to give me nicknames from cartoons and films. The one that always came back again and again was "Chaussettes", which came from the Kevin Costner movie Dances With Wolves. There was a wolf with white markings on his feet and my brothers decided to give me the same nickname, so I was "Socks".

Olivier Giroud

BEST CHILDHOOD MOMENT

The best moment was when my mother bought me a pair of Nike Mercurial Vapor football boots. I was 12 and I was very happy about it because we didn't have a lot of money and it was a real "wow" moment for me. Those boots were expensive and still my mother bought them for me because she knew I loved football. I will never forget this moment.

Antonio Rüdiger

FIRST POSITION

I was centre-forward for the school. I wasn't as big as I am now, I was quite small, so I wasn't a target man, but like every young boy I wanted to play in the position where you scored goals – a more glamorous position.

Gary Cahill

WORLD CUP QUIZ

These Blues stars all represented their countries at the 2018 World Cup, but can you remember which team each of them played for and spot the right flags?

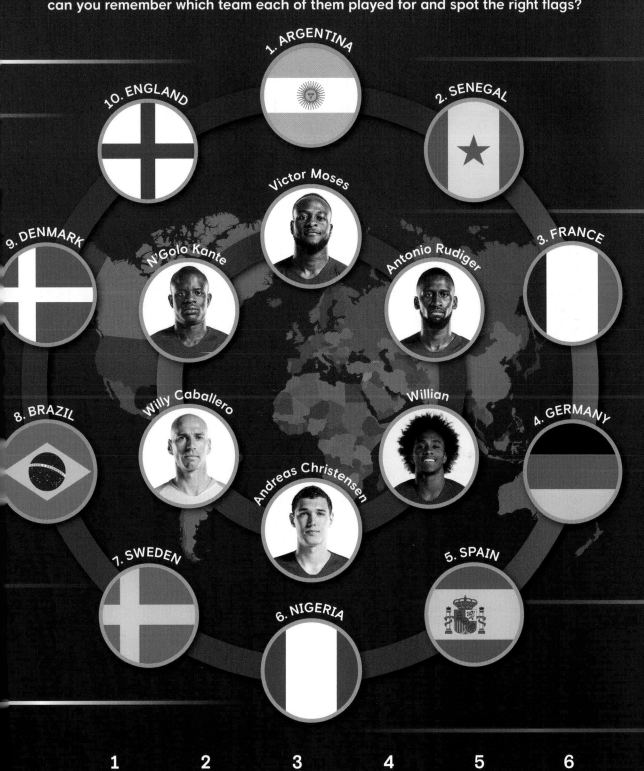

1. ARGENTINA

10. ENGLAND

2. SENEGAL

Victor Moses

9. DENMARK

N'Golo Kante

Antonio Rudiger

3. FRANCE

8. BRAZIL

Willy Caballero

Willian

4. GERMANY

Andreas Christensen

7. SWEDEN

5. SPAIN

6. NIGERIA

	1	2	3	4	5	6
PLAYER						
FLAG						

GOALS, GOALS, GOALS!

How well do you know Chelsea's recent goalscorers and their greatest hits?

1

Frank Lampard is Chelsea's all-time top goalscorer, but how many goals did he score for us in total?

A: 101 ☐   B: 181 ☐   C: 211 ☐

2

Chelsea Women reached the semi-final of the Champions League for the first time in 2018. Which player scored in the round of 16, the quarter-finals and the semi-finals?

A: Ji So-yun ☐   B: Fran Kirby ☐   C: Ramona Bachmann ☐

3

Chelsea scored 103 goals in all competitions last season, but how many of them were scored by Spanish players?

A: 16 ☐   B: 36 ☐   C: 56 ☐

4

Who scored the goal against West Bromwich Albion that clinched Chelsea the Premier League title in May 2017?

A: Gary Cahill ☐   B: John Terry ☐   C: Michy Batshuayi ☐

5

N'Golo Kanté was voted Chelsea's Player of the Season in 2017/18, but against whom did he score his only goal of the campaign?

A: Leicester City ☐   B: Manchester City ☐   C: Swansea City ☐

6

An amazing team move against Brighton won Chelsea's Goal of the Season in 2017/18, but who finished it off with a great strike from the edge of the area?

A: Willian ☐   B: Michy Batshuayi ☐   C: Eden Hazard ☐

7

Our Goal of the Season the previous year – 2016/17 – was an awesome solo effort against Arsenal, but who is pictured being mobbed after scoring it?

A: Pedro ☐   B: Eden Hazard ☐   C: Willian ☐

8

Which wing-back scored both goals in our 2-1 away win at Tottenham early last season?

A: Davide Zappacosta ☐   B: Victor Moses ☐   C: Marcos Alonso ☐

9

Who is pictured here celebrating one of his two goals in our 3-2 away win at Southampton last season?

A: Alvaro Morata ☐   B: Olivier Giroud ☐   C: Eden Hazard ☐

10

Can you name the player pictured with the WSL trophy who was part of Chelsea Women's double-winning teams in 2015 and 2018?

A: Hedvig Lindahl ☐   B: Millie Bright ☐   C: Carly Telford ☐

11

Alvaro Morata scored nine headed goals in 2017/18 and seven of them were set up by the same player. Who was it?

A: Cesar Azpilicueta ☐   B: Victor Moses ☐   C: Willian ☐

12

Who scored our only goal in the Champions League final against Bayern Munich in 2012 and then netted the winning penalty in the shootout?

A: Fernando Torres ☐   B: Frank Lampard ☐   C: Didier Drogba ☐

13

John Terry is Chelsea's top-scoring defender of all time with 67 goals, but against whom did he score his last Blues goal in May 2017?

A: West Ham ☐   B: West Brom ☐   C: Watford ☐

14

Chelsea's highest-scoring Premier League season came in 2009/10 when we bagged 103 on the way to winning the title, but how many of those were scored against Wigan Athletic on the last day of the season?

6 ☐   8 ☐   10 ☐

15

Let's see how well you know your history! After last season's triumph at Wembley, Chelsea have won the FA Cup eight times but only one Blues player has scored in every round on the way to lifting the famous old trophy. Who was it?

A: Gianfranco Zola ☐   B: Didier Drogba ☐   C: Peter Osgood ☐

SOCCER SCHOOLS

BOYS AND GIRLS OF ALL ABILITIES AGED 4-13 YEARS

Courses include
Mini Kickers | Advanced | Goalkeepers

———

Operating in Surrey, Berkshire, Middlesex, London, Essex, Hampshire, Wiltshire, Sussex & Kent

———

Visit chelseafc.com/foundation for your nearest venue

BLUES BARBERS

1

2

3

We feel like Eden Hazard has had the same haircut for a long time, so decided to give him some inspiration in case he felt like a change. But, can you work out which of his Chelsea team-mates' styles he is copying in each of these pictures?

4

5

6

BEHIND THE

David Luiz puts everything on the line to score in a fun training game using a giant ball and a tiny goal!

Pedro gets a perfect selfie when joining kids from our Hong Kong Soccer School for a kick-around at Cobham.

Summer signing Kepa Arrizabalaga gets a lesson on Chelsea's history from new Blues team-mate and fellow Spain international Cesar Azpilicueta on the goalkeeper's first day at Cobham.

Willy Caballero, Victor Moses, Pedro, Gary Cahill and Andreas Christensen make friends with a police officer on a visit to the Chelsea and Westminster Hospital near Stamford Bridge.

SCENES

Join us for a look at what the Chelsea players get up to behind the scenes at Cobham and on the road...

Marcos Alonso, Willian and David Luiz practice their popcorn catching skills while filming some online videos for fans.

Marcos Alonso, Willy Caballero, Pedro and Cesc Fàbregas pass the time by playing Ludo on the plane to France in pre-season.

Pedro, Callum Hudson-Odoi and Cesc Fàbregas show a couple of local sporting stars how to play real football on our trip to Australia.

Antonio Rüdiger makes sure the coaches know whose turn it is to do the fitness training next.

CHELSEA PLAYER

The Chelsea players, staff and supporters came together in west London for our traditional end-of-season awards ceremony in May. With our men's, women's and Academy teams all winning trophies last season, there was plenty to celebrate at the 2018 party, as our best players from across the club were invited on to the stage to collect their awards.

FAN FAVOURITE

The Blues supporters voted N'Golo Kanté as the 2018 Chelsea Player of the Year. The French midfielder was brilliant again during the 2017/18 season, picking up where he left off at the end of a debut campaign when he won our Players' Player of the Year award and pretty much every national award going. "Because I'm not the one who scores many goals, to be chosen by the fans for my season is something I have to appreciate and thank them for," said our No7. "The kind of player I am doesn't usually win all these awards, but I need to thank them for choosing me as Player of the Year for my game, for my work during the season."

DOUBLE DOUBLE

Awards seem to come in pairs for Willian, with 2018 bringing him our Players' Player of the Year and Goal of the Season trophies. It is the second time he has been chosen by his team-mates, also winning that award in 2016, which was another double year for him as he was chosen for the fans' award too. However, the 2018 Goal of the Season was more of a team effort, the Brazilian combining with Eden Hazard and Michy Batshuayi with a series of back heels to score against Brighton in the Premier League.

BREAKTHROUGH YEAR

Our 2018 Young Player of the Year was Andreas Christensen, a fitting reward after the defender returned from two years on loan in Germany and forced his way into the Chelsea first-team with some great performances. The Dane grabbed his opportunity with both hands, having been at the club since he was 16, and made 40 appearances in all competitions in 2017/18.

CLEAN SWEEP

There was no question who Chelsea Women's star performer was in 2017/18, as Fran Kirby was named as the Blues' Player of the Year by the fans and her team-mates, as well as already being chosen as English football's best female player by journalists and opponents. "It's been a perfect evening, I couldn't ask for any more really," said Kirby as she juggled all her awards. "I really pushed myself to the limits and it's definitely been my best season for Chelsea."

ONE FOR THE FUTURE

After a season when our Under-18s won all four competitions we entered, it is no surprise that team's captain was named Academy Player of the Year. Defender Reece James lifted the FA Youth Cup as skipper and played a key role in our other victories, making 42 appearances across our Academy sides, as well as being part of the development squad which reached the semi-finals of the Checkatrade Trophy. His form at youth level has been rewarded with a first season of first-team football, on loan with Wigan in the Championship for 2018/19.

THE YEAR 2018

PFA TEAM OF THE YEAR

Marcos Alonso was named in the Professional Footballers' Association Team of the Year for the first time in 2018, making him the 22nd player to be picked while representing Chelsea. The Spaniard will be hoping to make the selection again this season, joining a number of other Blues who have been chosen more than once.

To prove it, here is our own XI, made up just of former Chelsea players who have made the PFA Team of the Year at least twice...

PETR CECH

Big Pete is the only Chelsea goalkeeper ever to be selected in the PFA Team of the Year and received the honour twice – after winning his first Premier League title in 2005 and again in 2014.

BRANISLAV IVANOVIC

The stocky defender was a powerful presence at the back for nearly a decade at Stamford Bridge, being named in the PFA Team of the Year in the 2010 and 2015 title-winning campaigns.

JOHN TERRY

The former Blues skipper is one of only two men to have been named in the PFA Team of the Year four times as a Chelsea player, with Eden Hazard. Unsurprisingly, three came in seasons he captained us to the title – 2005, 2006 and 2015 – 2004 being the other.

WILLIAM GALLAS

Chelsea's back-to-back titles of 2004/05 and 2005/06 were built on one of the most solid defences the Premier League has ever seen, so it is no surprise Frenchman Gallas joined Terry in the Team of the Year for both those seasons.

ASHLEY COLE

The left-back's consistency is shown by the fact that he was named in the PFA Team of the Year four times, although only the last was with Chelsea. After three selections as an Arsenal player, he repeated the feat as a Blue in 2009/10.

FRANK LAMPARD

Among Lampard's many honours are three picks in the PFA Team of the Year. Even more impressive, they came in back-to-back from 2003/04 to 2005/06, all with Chelsea. He was also named PFA Fans' Player of the Year in 2005.

ANDY TOWNSEND

Townsend was named in the PFA Team of the Year in two of his three seasons with Chelsea – 1990/91 and 1991/92 – as well as once with Norwich in 1988/89.

GRAEME LE SAUX

The versatile left-sided player was first named in the PFA Team of the Year after helping Blackburn to claim the Premier League title in 1994/95. After returning for a second spell with Chelsea in 1997/98, his excellent first season back in SW6 saw him make the selection a second time.

NICOLAS ANELKA

The French forward's two appearances in the PFA Team of the Year came 10 years apart. The first was with Arsenal in 1999, when he was PFA Young Player of the Year, the second was in 2009, when he was the Premier League's top scorer with 19 goals for Chelsea.

KERRY DIXON

The Eighties icon is unique in this team, as he was named in the PFA Team of the Year in both the Second and First Divisions with Chelsea, in back-to-back seasons, after winning promotion in 1984 and scoring 24 goals on our return to the top flight in 1984/85.

DIDIER DROGBA

Drogba was named in the PFA Team of the Year in both seasons he won the Premier League Golden Boot award. He scored 20 goals in the league in 2006/07 and went even better with 29 in the 2009/10 Double-winning season.

SEE IT. HEAR IT. FEEL IT.

The all-new Chelsea FC museum and tour experience.
Get closer than ever before with exclusive content,
360 films and much more.

COMPETITION
WIN SIGNED CHELSEA SHIRTS!

We have signed shirts up for grabs from both the men's team and the Chelsea women's squad. Answer the below questions correctly for your chance to win.

MEN'S SHIRT

Who scored the winning goal in the 2018 FA Cup final at Wembley?

a) Cesar Azpilicueta   b) Eden Hazard   c) N'Golo Kante

Entry is by email only. Only one entry per contestant. Please enter CFC MEN followed by either A, B, or C in the subject line of an email. In the body of the email, please include your full name, address, postcode, email address, phone number and date of birth and send to: frontdesk@ grangecommunications.co.uk by Sunday 31st March 2019.

WOMEN'S SHIRT

Who won both the PFA and FWA Women's Player of the Year awards?

a) Ramona Bachmann   b) Erin Cuthbert   c) Fran Kirby

Entry is by email only. Only one entry per contestant. Please enter CFC WOMEN followed by either A, B, or C in the subject line of an email. In the body of the email, please include your full name, address, postcode, email address, phone number and date of birth and send to: frontdesk@ grangecommunications.co.uk by Sunday 31st March 2019.

Louis from Clevedon, 2018 Women's shirt competition winner.

Competition Terms and Conditions

1) The closing date for this competition is Sunday 31st March 2019 at midnight. Entries received after that time will not be counted.

2) Information on how to enter and on the prize form part of these conditions.

3) Entry is open to those residing in the UK only. If entrants are under 18, consent from a parent or guardian must be obtained and the parent or guardian must agree to these terms and conditions. If entrants are under 13, this consent must be given in writing from the parent or guardian with their full contact details.

4) This competition is not open to employees or their relatives of Chelsea Football Club. Any such entries will be invalid.

5) The start date for entries is 31st October 2018 at 4pm.

6) Entries must be strictly in accordance with these terms and conditions. Any entry not in strict accordance with these terms and conditions will be deemed to be invalid and no prize will be awarded in respect of such entry. By entering, all entrants will be deemed to accept these rules.

7) One (1) lucky winner will win a 2018/19 season signed men's football shirt and one (1) lucky winner will win a 2018/19 season signed women's football shirt.

8) The prize is non-transferable and no cash alternative will be offered. Entry is by email only. Only one entry per competition per contestant. Please enter CFC MEN (for the Men's Shirt Competition) or CFC WOMEN (for the Women's Shirt Competition) followed by either A, B or C in the subject line of an email. In the body of the email, please include your full name, address, postcode, email address and phone number and send to: frontdesk@ grangecommunications.co.uk by Sunday 31st March 2019.

9) The winner will be picked at random. The winner will be contacted within 72 hours of the closing date. Details of the winner can be requested after this time from the address below.

10) Entries must not be sent in through agents or third parties. No responsibility can be accepted for lost, delayed, incomplete, or for electronic entries or winning notifications that are not received or delivered. Any such entries will be deemed void.

11) The winner will have 72 hours to claim their prize once initial contact has been made by the Promoter. Failure to respond may result in forfeiture of the prize.

12) At Chelsea FC plc and our group companies, we go the extra mile to ensure that your personal information is kept secure and safe. We will not share your information with any other companies or use your data other than as necessary to administrate the competition. Once the competition is over your information will be securely destroyed. Your information will always be safeguarded under the terms and conditions of the Data Protection Act 1998 and CFC's Privacy Policy (https://www. chelseafc.com/en/footer/privacy-policy) to ensure that the information you provide is safe.

13) The Promoter reserves the right to withdraw or amend the promotion as necessary due to circumstances outside its reasonable control. The Promoter's decision on all matters is final and no correspondence will be entered into.

14) The Promoter (or any third party nominated by the Promoter) may contact the winner for promotional purposes without notice and without any fee being paid.

15) Chelsea Football Club's decision is final; no correspondence will be entered in to. Except in respect of death or personal injury resulting from any negligence of the Club, neither Chelsea Football Club nor any of its officers, employees or agents shall be responsible for (whether in tort, contract or otherwise):

   (i) any loss, damage or injury to you and/or any guest or to any property belonging to you or any guest in connection with this competition and/or the prize, resulting from any cause whatsoever;

   (ii) for any loss of profit, loss of use, loss of opportunity or any indirect, economic or consequential losses whatsoever.

16) This competition shall be governed by English law.

17) Promoter: Grange Communications Ltd, 22 Great King Street, Edinburgh EH3 6QH.

SPOT THE DIFFERENCE

Using your skill, can you spot the 10 differences between the two team pictures below?

Answers on p62

QUIZ ANSWERS

P20 WHO AM I?

1. Antonio Rudiger	6. Eden Hazard
2. Alvaro Morata	7. Cesar Azpilicueta
3. Pedro	8. Willian
4. Marco Alonso	9. Andreas Christensen
5. N'Golo Kante	10. Olivier Giroud

P50 GOALS, GOALS, GOALS

Q1 - C	Q4 - C	Q10 - A
Q2- A	Q5 - A	Q11 - A
Q3 - B (36 – Morata 15, Alonso 8, Pedro 7, Azpilicueta 3, Fàbregas 3.	Q6 - A	Q12 - C
	Q7 - B	Q13 - C
	Q8 - C	Q14 - B
	Q9 - B	Q15 - C

P30 FACT OR FICTION?

1. Fiction	6. Fiction
2. Fact	7. Fact
3. Fiction	8. Fact
4. Fact	9. Fiction
5. Fiction	10. Fact

P53 BLUES BARBERS

1 David Luiz	4 Willy Caballero
2 Emerson Palmieri	5 Willian
3 Callum Hudson-Odoi	6 Marcos Alonso

P49 WORLD CUP QUIZ

Willy Caballero – Argentina

Andreas Christensen – Denmark

Willian – Brazil

N'Golo Kanté – France

Victor Moses – Nigeria

Antonio Rüdiger – Germany

P61 SPOT THE DIFFERENCE